Magnitude

Magnitude

poems by
Deborah Seddon

Magnitude

Dryad Press (Pty) Ltd
Postnet Suite 281, Private Bag X16, Constantia, 7848,
Cape Town, South Africa
www.dryadpress.co.za / business@dryadpress.co.za

Copyright © poems Deborah Seddon
All rights reserved

No part of this book may be reproduced or transmitted in any form or by any electronic or mechanical means, including photocopying and recording, or any other information storage or retrieval system, without prior written permission from the publisher or copyright holder.

Cover design & typography: Stephen Symons
Copy Editor: Helena Janisch
Cover Image: *Where*, by Elize de Beer
2022, collograph and monotype 28cm x 46.5cm
Set in 9.5/14pt Palatino Linotype
First published in Cape Town by Dryad Press (Pty) Ltd, 2025

ISBN 978-1-0370-4468-7 (Print)
ISBN 978-1-0370-4469-4 (Electronic)

Visit www.dryadpress.co.za to read more about all our books and to buy them. You will also find features, links to author interviews and news of author events. Follow our social media platforms on Instagram and Facebook to be the first to hear about our new releases.

Dryad Press is supported by the Government of South Africa through the National Arts Council of South Africa (an agency of the Department of Arts & Culture), whose assistance is gratefully acknowledged.

Perhaps home is not a place but simply an irrevocable condition.
—James Baldwin

CONTENTS

I

Arrivals, Departures	3
The First Time	6
Harare City, Sunshine City	7
Living Will	10
Scratch That	13
Last Morning	20
Bella	22
Family Home	23
All the Words	25
Sisters	26
Smartphone	29
Visitations	30
How Long Has This Been Going On?	32
Baba	34
Grief Doesn't Come in Five Stages	36
Someday I'll Love Deborah Seddon	37
Miss Jackson	39
Template	41
Old Testament	42
No Mama, No Papa, No Whisky Soda	44
7 Balfour Road	50
Aftermath	51
Magnitude	52

II

O-o-h Child	57
South Africans Only	59
Sectioned	61
Reggae for Bob	64
Line in the Sand	66
Godson	68
Crackdown	70
Blueberries	71
History Will Break Your Heart	73
Crypsis	75
Pride	77
One Hundred Lesbians	79
We Are Mostly Water	84
Thin Line	86
I Know You Are Reading This Poem	87
The Song Of Deborah	89
Acknowledgements	91
Notes on Poems and Quotations	92

I

Arrivals, Departures

I have been flying away from
and towards you my entire adult life.

You never hid your grief.
Standing among strangers,

you covered my face with tears and kisses.
Tied little bows to the handles of my suitcase

that trundled around the carousel to greet me,
waving loops trapped in the zip's metal grin.

To be a mother is to be always letting go –

from the moment the child turns in the womb,
head engaged in the pelvic brim,

from the moment the contractions shudder
through the body like the pain of a torn-away limb.

*

When you grew old, I no longer let you
drive me to the airport.

Contained the pain at the gate of your house,
the waiting taxi's smoke idling into the dawn.

Harare. Johannesburg. Port Elizabeth. Makhanda.
Makhanda. Port Elizabeth. Johannesburg. Harare.

To leave you was to travel all day with our grief.

My heart hanging in the pit of my chest,
a dark well where the handle keeps spinning.

I hated the drive to P. E. airport. Our last ninety minutes
spent on a highway to meet your early morning plane.

Your face turned towards me in the passenger seat
to hand me a cup from our flask of sweet tea.

Watching you slip again through the check point to security.
Letting other people help you lift your case and coat.

Staying as close to you as I could 'til the plane left the ground.
Watching the runway from the restaurant with a coffee

until you filed across the tarmac with the other passengers,
your little four-wheeled red suitcase dragging behind you,

your bent head, your weeping visible from the high windows,
where I watch you climb the juddering staircase into the plane,

the clang of each step a return to your task of making
each day count in a house bereft of husband and children.

*

In those moments when you descended from planes,
with each considered step of your low-heeled pumps,

wheeling your little four-wheeled red suitcase ahead of you
on the hot tarmac, seeing me at last through the glass,

stopping to jump, smile, wave with both hands,
beginning to walk more quickly,

your mama beehive hairdo pushed to the back
of your head like a little crushed bird's nest,

you brought into my opening adult arms
everything you had loved in the child.

Your wet, red face creasing into joy and relief,
leaving damp spots on my cheeks, my shoulders and neck.

My heart tugged up hard above my head,
like a brand new kite on clean strings.

The First Time

With my small cardboard suitcase. My sandy-coloured sandals. My dress with the orange flower buttons that pop out at their middles. I know that I am five. I know how to unlatch the gate. I take my floppy cotton hat. An apple. Some juice and a book. I know the way to town.

Barton finds me sitting in the tall grass at the corner. Where my small road joins the big one. On the edge of the footpath that cuts through the feathery grass. Sand littered with bottle caps and stompies. My hands around my knees. In his starched white uniform he looks at me in silence. His outstretched hand is not a demand. We go back up the hill together.

Harare City, Sunshine City

You can ride all the way through the centre on Samora Machel with skyscrapers on either side. Except now it's called the A5. There are new roads and roundabouts. It's confusing. You could follow on Google maps except that Google maps doesn't know anything about the men with AK-47s on the corners by State House. How they can hiss and raise their guns a little higher when you stop at the robots (especially when you have a dog in the car). People call through their open car windows at the next robot. *Are you okay? What did he want? Do you think it was the dog?* Remember then, that the wrong turn home will always be right, down Josiah Tongogara. Better to go the other way, left down Herbert Chitepo, except that Google maps always calls him Herbert Chai-po and then you shout at the woman's voice on the phone.

Outside the new law offices that your father would have loved, you stop to buy a Biggie Bear banana-flavoured ice lolly from a Dairiboard ice cream vendor. He tells you through the smoke rising from the refrigerated box on the front of his bicycle that his name is Shame. You wonder what his mother was feeling at his birth and you say this. He laughs and shakes your hand. You take his picture and send it to him on WhatsApp.

There, on the corner, beside the huge chrome and copper sulphate blue employment insurance office that you do not even bother to visit, because the claim you could make to help pay for the funeral is not worth the time nor the paperwork. But don't the orange spathodea trees in flower everywhere look so pretty against the bright blue glass?

At the robots, at the corner of Herbert Chitepo and Simon Muzenda by the Sacred Heart Cathedral, you see Wilson again and feel like crying, because this time you have the pin to the EcoCash on your mother's phone. You yell out of the window, *Wilson! I'm back and I've got EcoCash!* The light goes green and he runs across the robots with you. You buy two enormous bags of unshelled monkey nuts. Wilson receives the EcoCash on a friend's phone. His has been stolen. In the photograph, his smiling grey-brown face says everything about what it means to live hawking monkey nuts at the robots next to the Cathedral of the Sacred Heart. His eyes are bloody. His hoodie is dirty and torn. So is his upper lip. But he says it again. Just as he did when you met him here before.

He holds up both bags, leans through the window, and says *Hello my sister, you know you want some.* You laugh together. You are so astonished to find yourself home and addressed in this fashion. You want to step out of the car and hug him hard, with the huge sad joy of being here again, on Herbert Chitepo with Wilson and his friends in the land of your birth. In the city of your youth.

There is the Ambassador Hotel, where the security guards chased you and your friends that night on the roof for playing drinking games. Your schoolgirl faces dotted with the soot of champagne corks as you slid down the fire escape and away. You slid away. You gave it all up. You know you can never live here again. You know that you are only playing at all this. Buying yourself ice cream and monkey nuts in the drive time between doctors and lawyers.

On Samora Machel, you can drive straight down the middle of the small patch of skyscrapers. Past the curved beauty of the Monomatapa Hotel, the gold B&H box of the Sheraton. The stone chameleon and the praying mantis at the Museum of Human Sciences. You can drive straight through in one day to the fever trees and sweat of Lake Kariba. Barefoot. In shorts. To sing every Freddie Mercury song aloud together under the stars the night he died.

Living Will

They make us all feel better,
these dysfunctional American lives.
Not a tree in sight!
Every Sunday night, as the camera pans over Southfork Ranch
in the opening credits, you suck your teeth
and can be counted upon to utter the same pronouncement
on the living arrangements of Texan millionaires.
First you chased me back to bed, away from the evil J.R.
and the alcoholic Sue Ellen. Alexis Carrington returned
to haunt her ex and his new wife (one of them driven crazy
when the walls of the offices are coated in toxic paint).
Then I was old enough to sit right next to you
on the couch instead of peeping in secret
from under the table in the dining room.

Given a hospital scene – the family gathered
around the bed of a loved one kept alive with oxygen
mask and machines, the room full of feeding tubes,
beeps and screens – you reach for my hand
without turning your face from the television,
give it a squeeze and a shake for emphasis:
I don't ever want that, do you hear me, to be kept
going on life support like that.

You'd seen it with your only brother, 19, his shaved head
bandaged to bind up the cracks in his skull, reaching
his unseeing hands across the bed in search of yours.
I don't ever want to be kept alive as a vegetable.

When life in the mines finally killed granddad,
black fungus of tuberculosis spreading across
the walls of his lungs, *his trachea* (you said it as you wept,
sitting on my bedroom floor as I played with your brother's
Mechano set, fixing a bendy straw into place as the chimney
for my train) *split like an old perished pipe.*

But there is no way we can switch off this stroke.
It has split you in two. The left side moves
but the ponderous right will do nobody's bidding.
Not even yours.

You give me power of attorney with your thumbprint.

Sitting up in your hospital bed for your lawyer
all determined and focused as if this is just a temporary
inconvenience. Each day in the hospital, I keep your living
will folded at the ready in the back pocket of my jeans.

You make me write it on the white board above your head:
ALLERGIC TO STRAWBERRIES.
NO ARTIFICIAL LIFE SUPPORT.

I direct that I be allowed to die and not be kept alive by artificial means
and I specifically reject any electrical or mechanical methods
of treatment aimed at prolonging or sustaining my life.

We are learning patience, you and I.
Neither of us has ever had it and now we need it most.

You will not listen. Will not hold your right arm for safety

in your left when we lift you out of bed each day to sit
upright in a chair. Insist on using your good arm, insist
that you lift yourself up, while the ragdoll right arm bucks
and swings until I shout that you are going to injure it all,
even the parts that work.

Why do you, I yell, *always have to be so again-est?*
But I know why, because we are the same, you and I.
You may just be the only person who is more again-est than me.

I think it was the borrowed wheelchair that did it. The day I
set it up you were gone. I think you took one look at the life
that lay ahead and refused. You never sat in it. Instead you
said you needed sleep.

Inside your dream you found your own way out
        slipped the noose of the body
                that had failed you

      shipped out for somewhere you could be alive
again and whole

a spirit deliberate and certain   striding away from all of us

                into the wayward dark

Scratch That

I was in the house when it happened. It happened while I slept. I lay down on the couch.

I slept like the dead. On a hot Sunday afternoon in March, I rolled in among the cushions.

*

I wake up cold. On that hot day in March on a Sunday afternoon. The wind chime on the stoep. The birdsong. The birds. I walk down the passage. Thuli, the nurse, sits quiet in her chair, reading. She stirs and smiles as I enter the bedroom. *How is she*? I ask. *She's fine, she's sleeping.* We smile at each other.

I like her. This calm gentle woman who makes my mother laugh. Who teases that my mother will be dancing at her wedding in August. I reach for my mother's sleeping face on the pillows. I brush her hair from her forehead. Cold. She isn't breathing. She is cold.

*

I lay down for an hour. I lay down for just an hour. On a hot Sunday afternoon in March. I slept for the first time since I'd arrived. I was in the house when it happened. I brush her hair from her forehead. She is cold. I put my mouth over hers. I put my mouth over hers and blow my breath into her mouth. My fists pump her chest.

*

I blow my breath into her mouth. I shout. My fists pump
her chest. I cry. Thuli cries. I phone the doctor. I phone
the ambulance. The ambulance doesn't answer. I phone
a friend. I shout. I pump her chest. My breath blows
into her mouth.

*

The doctor arrives. The six-foot doctor with his hairy chest.
He leans over her. He puts his stethoscope to her chest and
listens for her heart. *No*, he says, *she's gone*. I shout again *no,
no, no, no, no, no!* He tells the ambulance not to come. I do
something I have never done. I sit next to my mother in her bed
and I smoke. The masahwira arrive. One friend. Then another.
They hold me as I weep. They talk to me. I talk to them.
The night comes on in this blur of conversation.

*

The news of her collapse arrives and keeps arriving, as I book
my ticket, pack my bag. The calls and calls from her friends,
telling me about my mother, the ambulance, the hospital.
She can't speak Debs, I think it's quite bad. She can't speak. I take
a black shirt out of my cupboard. I hold it up and throw it back.
No, I say to the shirt, *I don't need you. I am not going to a funeral.*
Most of the clothes I pack are dirty. Taken from the basket
in the bathroom I'd planned to wash that weekend. I start
packing and I do not sleep.

*

My tall broad mother sits in the hospital bed like a little puppet
with her strings cut. Her gasp as she turns her head toward me
and opens her eyes to my voice is her gasp. Then the rush

to speak herself to me as she has always done hits the slack sag
of lips without nerves. Hiss and teeth and repetition. The left
side pressing forward to help. The effort. Just to shape her lips
around the same old words. To lift the sag at the right corner
of her mouth. All the old shapes lost. She cannot smile but
I can tell she is happy I'm here. Her beautiful and very
important hair is ragged. She cannot move and her voice
is a breathy frustrated riddle. I watch her face. Her eyes
are wild. She cannot keep still. Fighting against her immobility
and silence. Fighting so hard she cannot breathe.

*

Lying in the spare room at my best friend's house, I want to be
in the hospital. I want to smoke at three in the morning. I want
to be in the hospital with my mother. I want to smoke. But
there is no way out. No way past all the armed and alarmed
doors and windows. I roll towels under the door and puff out
of the window. I want to smoke. So they give me the key
to their generator cage. I stand out there smoking at night next
to the petrol-driven thump. One spark from my cigarette
and we'll all blow. All that time the night jar cries and cries.
My mother called it her death bird. The night jar who sang
under her college window every night that term until her
brother died.

*

Tiny little traps or gaps in time. We fall into them. Like a needle
trapped in the scratch on a record. Living inside the bit that's
missing. I can't even remember the name of the hospital but
I am still sitting there in the foyer. With a huge picture
of Emmerson Mnangagwa hanging over us all. It's dark.
The night air on the pavement has its autumn chill. There

is so much activity inside. Too much noise. People wander in
and out from the street. Shouting and banging. Trolleys and
bedpans. This hospital sounds like a riot. But no one is visiting
anyone. I find it impossible to understand why I cannot be
allowed to simply sit beside her. In the ward where she lies
above me. Listening to all this. Unsleeping. Unable to get out of
bed. Unable to call out for help. Exactly one floor above my head.

*

Just above my head. My mother lies just above my head on the
next floor. The matron of the ward would not let me stay.
My mother who was so hungry she pulled herself up by the
bars of the bed and roared. In twenty-four hours, I will move
her somewhere else, to the cool quiet wards of the Avenues
Clinic. In seventy-two hours, Evelyn the night nurse will arrive
in her sleeveless blue jersey. Just by being there, she will make
everything calm. But now I am thirsty and my mother is
roaring somewhere just above my head.

*

It is after visiting hours. The ward matron will not allow me
to stay. I have asked her quietly three times. I am thirsty and
tired. I haven't slept since I got the call. Yesterday. In another
country. I am texting my best friend for a lift home while
staring at the empty water cooler and the dirty blue plastic
cups piled around it.

*

I have to keep telling that woman who is still sitting in the hospital foyer that she moved her mother out by lunchtime of the next day. That they couldn't take her anywhere better because no one had the US dollar cash needed for admission elsewhere.

*

One of her best friends hunches over her kitchen counter and tells me that she had taken the wrong envelope. She had her salary in one and her grocery money in the other. In her rush to meet the ambulance, she had taken the money for her groceries. It wasn't enough. *It's alright,* I say. She weeps with my arm around her shoulders. I am not the only one who stays sitting in the foyer of the only hospital anyone could afford in US dollar cash that day. No one should have to be stuck in such a place.

*

I am still sitting in the foyer of the hospital when I am taken by friends to see an improv show at Reps Theatre. It is a Friday. This is what they are doing this evening. I am their guest and life goes on. I am still sitting in the hospital foyer or wishing to be on the floor above it when I sit in the audience gripping a plastic tumbler of gin and tonic. All around me people are laughing so hard they twist and rock their bodies in their chairs and wave their hands in the air. I think about that improv now. I wonder, was it really that terrible? Yes. It was really that terrible. So bad, in fact, it deserved the words Jack Nicholson says to Shirley MacLaine in *Terms of Endearment* when she asks him if he wants to come in: *I would rather stick needles in my eyes.*

My school friends and I have used this phrase since 1985.
The film was released in 1983. We saw it two years later, our first year of high school, because that was how long the movies took to reach us in Zimbabwe.

*

You are my mother and you are death. You have become death. Because of you, I have never known it so close. I have slept beside it on the pillow and kissed its cold soft forehead. I have combed its dark and tangled hair.

*

You are so alike, say my friends. She's nothing like me, I think. But our road rage is identical. Who am I? Who is anyone?

*

When I was a small girl, I fell down a hole my mother had dug for a palm tree. Correction: I fell down a hole she had *ordered* dug for a palm tree. I was in the hole the entire afternoon. I couldn't climb out. The soil walls crumbled under me, pushed me back down. I felt like a beetle in an ant lion pit. I knew how to trick them. How to lie in the dirt and spit in their holes to catch them. Now I was the meal in an ant lion pit. I just sat in the dirt and waited.

Lamrik the gardener found me. He laughed at the small dirty child sitting in a hole in the soil. I laughed with him as he doubled over in his laughter. Lamrik had spent the whole day digging for my mother and weeding her garden but he still had the strength to lift me out.

*

I need you to lift me, Sekuru. I need you to lift me out. I want to sit with you again on a low wooden stool on the stoep of your house. I want to sit at your fire and sing with you as your fingers pluck the fishing wire strings of your guitar. Your guitar of green and gold. Handmade from a big square tin of Olivine oil. A circle of sound sliced into the centre. Teach me those words again, please Sekuru, sing them again and lift me up.
Swing low, sweet chariot, coming for to carry me home.

Last Morning

I wake beside you. The dark thinning.
You will never see this sun.
I take up plastic basin and warm water,
facecloth and soap.
Turn you over in my hands.
Climb over you like an ant, like a child.
Lift you like the woman I have become.

You are still my mother.
Heavier like this. Every limb flops now
like that stricken right side.

If I let go, if you land oddly,
I am afraid I may snap you.
But I have chosen to do this.

Sweat slicks my face, drops from my hairline,
runs from the pits of my arms.
I lie on the carpet.
Tears pool in my ears.
But I go back to you. I am thorough.

I wash between each creased and freckled finger.
The short modest nails.
The groove where your wedding ring rests.
You never took it off, not once.
Not even for surgery.

We will bury her with it,
I tell the two men in their white coats.

I watch the slow movement of blood
under your skin, as I turn you.
I am afraid I will disturb
the perfect peace of your face.
I do not want to leave you blotchy or lopsided.

I want you beautiful.
Sent out in a fresh, ironed nightgown.
Cream on your face.
Perfume in your hair.
This is my only prayer.

Your knees still bend, and your elbows.
But I can feel death taking you from me.
Your swift laughing capable body
stiffening like plaster under my hands.

I am hours at this task.
I have washed, rubbed, oiled these feet,
these baby toes which both tuck in, next to the rest.

These raspy heels.
These high-strung arches.
These carefully shaven legs.
These durable sun-damaged arms.

On your belly, I wipe the length
of your thick liver-coloured scar,

the wound where we were born, where they lifted us
out into the light.

Bella

She didn't want any more injections. When the vet left, I lay on the carpet, smoothing her snarl, closing her eyes. I held her and wailed. My tears dampened her whitened fur. I stroked her until the warmth left her body. This was once death for every family. To die at home. Laid out to be washed on a table in the house. I washed my mother's body. I shocked some friends. They had not wished to see or touch their parents after death.

I could choose an end for my dog. I held her in my arms all night, knowing morning would bring mercy, release. Most people are not as lucky. It took me two days to dig a deep enough grave. Wrap her in a sheet, place her in the earth, shovel it over her. I needed to keep her with me for a while. Her heart had stopped in ten seconds.

It took me two days to let her go. Put her in the ground. Listen gladly to rain falling over the garden, soaking her hair and skin. Think of her turning into part of the earth. Food for insects and plants. I want to be wrapped in a cotton sheet, laid in the soil. If I cannot have this, I want to be burnt. The idea of a coffin is disgusting. To rot all alone in a box. The final prison.

I wanted my mother. I wanted her voice and comfort. There is no comfort now. My mother and my dog are dead. The other little dog and I are so silent and bewildered together.

Family Home

There is a purple pin pushed deep into the felt of your
tomato-shaped pin cushion in the drawer under the bed
where no one ever vacuums.

In the cupboard in the passage there is a carton of Leopard
matches that cost $52 000.

In the liquor cabinet a bottle of bitters for $65 000.

In my bedroom cupboard a cake tin full of plastic hair
curlers, hair pins, an invitation to my parents' wedding,
and a little note from my grandmother to my great-aunt:
Baie, baie dankie, dat jy my hare so mooi gedoen het.

A bottle of Holy Water labelled HOLY WATER.
Cardboard boxes labelled CARDBOARD BOXES.
A big Mazoe Orange Crush bottle filled up with grit
to scour the pots when nobody could buy any Vim.

A bottle of calamine lotion. The white liquid set solid
at the bottom. You kept a bottle of the lotion
you once dabbed all over my small-girl body.

The chalky chemical smell as the cotton wool was soaked
and squeezed to cool red welts rising up under
my skin because once I was allergic to everything.

You kept the junket tablets and 20 tiny bottles
of food colouring you used to make our cakes.
My father's red Christmas shirt labelled
CHRIS CHRISTMAS SHIRT.

I lie in bed one whole morning to listen to a CD labelled
CHRIS'S VOICE – hear him firing off legal letters on his
dictaphone without even a pause between one missive and
the next – *We are, not unnaturally, more than a little vexed* …

What is this? I ask. Handing over, to your old friend,
an object fashioned from leather and string.

Oh, those were our dogtags, he says.
He stretches them over my head,
fastens the ties around my neck.

All the words

on the birthday cards and shopping lists and letters
all the bills and emails and envelopes and aerogrammes

little notes you'd left me long ago next to the kettle
to read when I came home from out dancing late

they all begin and end the same
Dearest Darling Debs   from your Everloving Mummy

words inside your notebooks
every wish and prayer and plan

years and years and years of our words
folded up in drawers and cupboards and passageways

you left your messages everywhere knowing this would
be my task – to find them out and burn them up

all the words churning above us now
in the air over the roof

rising with the smoke every night
mingling in the green and orange flames

the sweet dark brandy sleep
every night on the carpet next to the fire

waking to the call of the spookvoël
a green ghost crying into the dawn

Sisters

Cut a large aloe leaf at the base with a penknife.
Cut several large aloe leaves.

Make a hole in the head of each with a sharpened stick,
then string them together for ease of carrying.

These will be our fish.

We will slice them down the middle,
carve out and eat the bitter transparent flesh.

We will taste it with herbs and sometimes with peas
cooked over a fire made from the flowers of spathodea trees.

Later, when their seedpods crack, they will shape into perfect
boats to crest over the bubbling fountain into the pool

where the razor-bite leaves of the spikey palm
are sharks that swim among us.

Red waterberries cram tart in our mouths
but we have to be secretive about the peas.

If we are found eating peas – whole, green, sweet, squeaky,
delicious – we will be smacked.

We are also forbidden from scaring the chickens where
they sit in the straw in their dark shit stink of a coop,

but we are choosing among them one
to be our golden-feathered phoenix.

We climb into the smooth branched tunnel
of the red hibiscus hedge – it is our road to Golgotha.

We hang there till our arms hurt,
till we cry out from the pain.

We call out from the tangled interior as a friend arrives for tea:
Hello Mrs Watson! We're being crucified today!

We throw ourselves into piles of spathodea flowers,
to thrash and moan as we burn alive,

children cast into the fire
by the evil king Nebuchadnezzar.

White maggots feast in the flesh of vrot guavas.
These make the perfect hand grenades.

We jump from the roof of the hut with plastic bags as parachutes
and ride our hobby horses through leaf mould in the flower beds.

We are soldiers, pirates, outlaws, braves.

I am the man from Snowy River. You are the girl
who must wrest herself free before the ropes catch fire.

Our grandmother lives in the purple petrea bush, at the arch
by the gate, in its hardy fuzzy leaves, its helicopter flowers.

She also lives in her purple hibiscus,
the centre all scarlet and the palest of yellows.

Our great-grandmother's roses shake their petal rain
onto the polished slate of the stoep.

We drive hairy caterpillars inside dinky cars
in the sand pit. We sleep on the lawn in a tent.

We sit astride branches singing and riding our horses.
We sleep top to toe in our grey blanket hammock.

We eat of the fruit of this garden.
We purple all day in its mulberry trees.

We are covered in ants from the loquat tree.
They bite sticky yellow juice from our fingers and faces.

We are handed half a lemon each to rub our bodies of purple.
We stand naked at the kitchen door under the spray of the hose

before we are allowed back inside.

Smartphone

I've looked and looked,
said my mother,
for that little bear to send you,
the one who gives you a hug,
but I couldn't find him.
You won't find him mum, I said,
he's in Skype, not WhatsApp,
he's in another programme.
Oh I see, she said,
but I did find the face of a bear,
did you see him in my message?
Yes, I did, I said, well done
for finding him.
So I thought, she said, *that he*
could be our hug in WhatsApp,
is that okay?
Yes mum, I said,
that's wonderful.

Visitations

Sliding for cover right in front of my toes.
A snake on the night driveway.
Its long pale ribcage undulating in torchlight.

The day we bring you home from hospital,
there's an exhausted pigeon in the kitchen,
crouched on the worn formica tile next to the red pedal-bin,
identification bracelet clasped to one clawed foot.
I hide her in the leafy flowerbed with a bowl of honey water.

She's lost, let her rest, drink.
She'll die where she is, or recover her strength to fly.

The mortuary men will not let me watch
while they lift you from the bed to wheel you from the house.
It is distressing for the family, they advise.

They stand beside their trolley, terrified
of something in me that threatens to cry out.
Like a beast, like a strange, unknowable bird.
Like the night jar who threatened your dreams.

So I am sitting on the back kitchen steps with a cup of tea,
when the black beetle flies up the passage,
claps me on my shoulder, pats me on the head.
Disappearing with a whir into the bright blue hands of the air.

You are shedding your skin.
You are trying to get home –
*be ye therefore wise as serpents,
and harmless as doves.*

Your last night on earth, a gogga comes in through the window,
I think he is a flying ant until we raise our heads to watch
those glorious blue wings tap dance on the ceiling.
Dragonflies don't fly at night.

Here is my father in his glittering blue coat –
come to Fred and Ginger you up the silver staircase
to the moon.

How Long Has This Been Going On?

I could cry salty tears
Where have I been all these years?
Little wow, tell me now
How long has this been going on?
                – George and Ira Gershwin

In my favourite wedding photograph
(snapped through the windscreen
as they are leaving the church),
they are looking only at each other.

He is all insignia, epaulettes and hair oil.
She is satin in cream, tiara and pearls.
Her wide seductive laugh.
His bespectacled grin.
I love his look of boyish rapture –
he cannot quite believe this woman is his wife.
What a badass, what a darling, what a Bond girl.

They never quite lost it, whatever they shared
in this first look between them. That last holiday
together, when I joined them in Durban
a year before his death,
she giggled in the sun on the verandah
and scanned the horizon for ships,
while he cooked us kippers and eggs.
The salt air alive with the frisson of honeymoon.

When I was a child I liked to lie in bed
and hold back sleep, listen to the murmur
of their voices intertwined
on the other side of the wall.
Talking, laughing low,
that music made between them fanning out
into the safest place in the world.

Baba

You were as soft as your feet.
As soft as your song of *the fair hippopotami maid*
but there was never *mud, mud, glorious mud* between your toes.
You never went barefoot. Wore a pair of leather slippers
to walk the short walk across drought-withered grass to the pool.
A quiet man in a house full of noisy woebegone women.
Yammering and slamming doors. I cajoled, complained
that you would kill us all, each time you lit up in the car.
If I had been you, I would have left me at the side of the road.
You gave it up for my sake but the cancer got you anyway.

Oh Daddy Cool, you gave me Boney M.
Flanders and Swann. *Porgy and Bess.*
I like a Gershwin tune, how about you? You gave me jazz.
Louis Armstrong and Louis Prima. *Buona sera, signorina, kiss me goodnight.* I thought you made up the funny words
of all those songs you sang us as children. *Shadrack, Meshach and Abednego, into the fiery furnace, they did go.*

Fair enough, it's a considered position. That was your response
to my refusal of a British passport at sixteen. You did not
insist I see it your way. I never changed my mind.

> *Dad, if I could take all the English blood out of my body,*
> *I'd do it. These people invented concentration*
> *camps. I will never swear allegiance to the Queen.*
> *I will never bear the passport of a country that has*
> *brought down more evil on the world*
> *than everyone else put together.*

You died in harness, pacing like a shire horse,
dictating a letter to your secretary, composing words
in air like Henry James. Stopped,
caught your breath, a hand to your chest.
Your big knees and hairy hooves keeling under you
in a long slow bend towards your office floor. Dead
before the ambulance arrived,
before my mother reached you,
blind to your pale green walls, your acres of documents
in the IN and OUT trays, stacked on every filing cabinet
and piled on each of the chairs.

Perhaps you are too young to understand this, says your friend.
But he was lucky. He had a good death. I sit with him on the stoep
(missing you somewhere inside this lunchtime offering me a
gin – *with a little pink*).

This man sitting opposite me is not my father.
He means me no harm, but he is neither capable
nor willing to consider my position.

I want to carry you to the end of your journey,
to shoulder you out as you had shouldered me in.
But no, no, my girlie, he tuts. *You cannot be a pallbearer.
That is a job for the men.*

Grief Doesn't Come in Five Stages

Grief is a mess
you need to keep wiping up.
A troll with a spade
lurking to wallop you in doorways.
An ambush, a panic attack,
while waiting at a boiling kettle.
Yesterday you were angry all over again.
Today it was dark when you woke.
You pulled on a woolly hat
and got back into bed, wept.
Because you miss your mother
but also you fear you've become her –
an old woman going to bed in a woolly hat
because she is all alone and it is so cold.
Jy huil. Jy huil. It is clearer in her language.
The sky pebbling the ground with frozen hurt.
Perhaps you are the one who has died.
Perhaps her death has killed you.

Someday I'll Love Deborah Seddon

– after Ocean Vuong / after Roger Reeves / after Frank O'Hara

Someday I'll love the woman who
came out of that child.

A small stick, whittled down,
still green, pliable,

seated in a puddle of her own shame
because she is too afraid to ask

the sweet Miss Jackson out loud
if she can go to the toilet please.

Sometimes it feels
as if I might sit there forever

as my classmates whisper their questions
across the crayons.

Why didn't I ask before?
What am I going to do now?

Miss Jackson has dark curly hair.
She leads us in songs in the hall.

She sits so far away, too far away to get up.
If I get up everyone will see the back of my dress.

I have always been afraid. When I have spoken
through it, the shame has spread anyway,

dark and wide enough
to drown in.

One day I'll love Deborah Seddon.
One day I'll love that child

in the red Snoopy shirt
her father sent her in the post

playing with her football
on the spikey winter grass

so that she will be the first thing he sees
as the truck comes down the driveway

to bring him back from the bush
where he has been sent again on call-up.

The little girl who lived
in a puddle of her own shame.

The woman who found a scrapbook full of postcards
her daddy sent her from the war.

He couldn't tell her where he was
but he could ask of her,

Take good care of Mummy and your sister,
before she could even read.

Miss Jackson

The strangest thing is that Miss Jackson,
on our first day in her classroom,
stuck up a big picture on the board
of a little girl with muddy knees
holding a big bunch of carrots.

She taught us to read our first word:

LOOK!

She drew in the eyes –
a wide open pupil
into each of the Os – and we,
her wide staring pupils, we

fell in love
(at least I did)

LOOK!

The word enacts itself on the page.
So began a search that lasted years.

The word for train can be given wheels,
the small circle of the i makes the steam
to puff it off the page.

The P and L of an aeroplane give it wings to fly.

But LOOK!

The little girl who likes Miss Jackson,
with her wide skirts and curly hair,
is sitting in a puddle of her own making

even though she is already five.

LOOK!

The little girl who likes Miss Jackson
is too scared for words.

She cannot find her feet.
She cannot push out her chair.
She cannot put up her hand to ask.
She cannot wait anymore.
She cannot hold it in.

Template

Plates in the warming drawer kept warm or not kept warm
enough. Plates for ordinary and plates for best.
Plates kept all year in the cupboard
brought out only for guests.
The ordinary notwarmenough plates
flying across the dining room –
you want hot plates? I'll give you hot plates!
Your little flying saucers smash like exclamation points
as they hit against the walls.

The hands flying across the table. The spilt gravy
on the tablecloth a tragedy from which no one might
ever recover.

She spills her egg – the orange yolk bleeding – and he slaps
the side of her small head. Pigtails flaring.

In one deft reply, you stand and smash his glasses onto his face.
He sits at the head of the table staring through fractured lenses.

There is value in such teachings and I am thankful.
He hit you only once and you hit him so hard you broke
three of his ribs. He never hits us again. He sometimes grits
his teeth and raises up the flat of his hand.

But your bite is as bad as your bark. Your hackles on edge,
you bare your teeth and snarl and warn as you strike
your blinding arc in a circle all round us.
So no one will ever get in there and harm us.

Except you.

Old Testament

The obedient father and his son,
climbing with a backload of branches
to the altar on the mountainside.

> The boy asks, *but where is the lamb*
> *for a burnt offering?*

Did he kick? Did he struggle?
Did he cry out and plead? Did he beg
his father not to –

> as Abraham bound his wrists and ankles,
> hoisted him onto the altar,
> held him down and took up the knife
> to slay his only son?

Seated on a hard church pew
beside my obedient mother,
my little-girl-questions
the first to slip the knots that tied me down.

> *Would she?* I asked myself.
> *If God asked her, would my mother do the same?*
> *Would she sacrifice me?*

I found out at fourteen.

She turned around,
the pale pink powder on her face
still in her eyebrows,

her perfume in the air,
using her brush to punctuate each word.

Seated in her dressing gown,
she turned around
on the dressing table stool from the mirror
to look at me sitting on the bed.
She chose her words with care.

To say to her fourteen-year-old child –

> *I know what you are.*
> *I know what you are*
> *and I won't have it.*
> *I can't love it.*
> *You revolt me.*

All I could do was deny it. I wasn't lying.
I didn't know myself. Found out
before I was found. Told not to love
before I could love. Turned in against my desire
before I could listen to it sing.

Twenty-five years
before I made love to a woman.

> She sentenced me to twenty-five years.

A precise and artful targeting –
to pinch out just the tips
of the plant. Crushed
between forefinger and thumb.
The making impossible of either petal
or seed.

No Mama, No Papa, No Whisky Soda

Seizing his chance, a barefoot beggar-boy ran beside the Packard.
He drummed his fists on the doors and held out his palm to Jim,
shouting the street cry of all Shanghai:
'No mama! No papa! No whisky soda!'
  – J.G. Ballard, Empire of the Sun

>We are all penga here.
>No mama. No papa. No whisky soda.
>No Zesa. No petrol. No Coca-Cola.

I am cutting my brandy with Pepsi tonight. It's four months in, and it is all I can do, serious, ser-i-ous, not to take each of the new red metal chigubs I bought to feed the generator from the only two petrol stations in town that use US dollar coupons, but will no longer fill the plastic ones. Not to take every single one, and pour them round the perimeter of the house. As if laying down poison for ants.

>*Chigub, chigub, chigub.*

Then set it all ablaze, little Firestarter, stand back and watch it burn.

>*I heard somebody say*
>*Burn, baby, burn. Disco inferno.*
>*Burn, baby, burn. Burn that mother down.*

It's all I can do not to go all Stephen King on myself. I half expect
to find a rabid dog in the garage coz governments and Empires
fucked with my parents, left them holding on tightly
to everything they bought or owned for fifty years,
just in case they needed it one day. Until the old house
moulders like Miss Havisham's wedding cake in its stasis,
excess and deprivation.

> *Maswera sei?*
> *Taswera kana maswerawo.*

Everything they possessed black-bagged up. Labelled
with duct tape and permanent marker: clothes, shoes, sheets,
towels, pillows, blankets, books and toys divided between
the Children's Home, Hospice, old age charities, schools,
cyclone survivors and prisons. Because so many people
have almost nothing.

> *Are you fine?*
> *How can I be fine if you are not fine?*

I swing my solar lantern down the passage of the house. A bee
tied to the light as I walk from kitchen to bedroom like Ophelia
going to her muddy death, singing snatches of old songs.

> *She's crazy like a fool*
> *What about Daddy Cool?*

Today we cut down the pecan nut tree my father planted at my
birth. It has stood dead in the yard for years. Dhererai said we
should take it down before it falls. *Yes,* I said, *and if you have a
friend who can do it call him.* Fifteen minutes later, three men are
in the back garden with a chainsaw and ropes, cutting it branch
by branch.

> *Maiwe!*
> *Ndinopenga. Tinopenga.*
> *Maningi sterrek!*

A school friend arrives who has quit her antidepressants. Her husband and children don't approve. We sit in the empty sandpit smoking among naked Sindy and Ken dolls drying out on hot bricks. I have washed them in buckets of bleach. Salvaged from boxes of toys in the back hut covered in rat shit and the entire line is hanging with the clothes I washed when water got delivered over the wall.

> *Hey kid, would you like a Hershey bar?*
> *So would I.*

My father's clothes left hanging or folded in the cupboard for ten years without help or salvation. This is Harare, where if you don't iron every seam, every crease, you'll hatch putsi fly grubs from your arms where they laid their eggs in your sleeves. Ten years these beautiful clothes were left to face the goggas. I cannot even give them away until I wash them. Now they are all hanging on the line full of holes.

> *But I cannot choose but weep,*
> *to think they should lay him i' the cold ground.*

The trunk is coming down. I run towards it. The tree he planted that once stood for me.

> *Awake, awake, Deborah!*
> *Awake, awake, utter a song!*

My frame can't take it. It crashes and shatters into a hundred
pieces of very viable firewood all over the grass. We all sit on the
broken brought-down trunk. I take photographs of
everyone and the hairy brown caterpillars as big as my hand
who have made their homes in the rotten wood.

> Dead Woman Standing.
> *They all fall down.*

We read *Empire of the Sun* for O Level in a hot classroom in
Zimbabwe on a Wednesday afternoon with a syllabus
written in Cambridge. Our exams were marked in England
too. We still have the words in our heads.

> Children of hondo.
> Children of flight.
> This one goes out to the diaspora tonight.

Zesa is the Zimbabwe Electricity Supply Authority,
although supply is a contested word. Municipal water
stopped coming through the taps twenty years ago.
The borehole is dry so water comes from pipes on the
bowsers that deliver over the wall to the big green tank.

> No water. No sadza. No ATMs.
> No Twitter? No WhatsApp? Get a VPN.

She should be asleep, this bee, who flies with the solar
lantern swinging from my arm as if tied to the light that
floats and sways beneath photographs framed on the walls
of the passage.

> *How do you hold a moonbeam*
> *in your hand?*

She named me well, for here I am, drunk in the dark,
busy bee, still working on these drawers, these cupboards,
burning all the candles I can find. The perfume still pouring
from her bedroom cupboard. This is the third night
the doors have stood open to release her perfume from
the garments before I can handle her clothes.

> *My darling, your daddy*
> *has been dead for ten years now.*

My supper cooks in a pan on the one-plate gas cooker.
Lit by blue flame, carefully frozen kippers dissolve in oil.
Salt smoke drifts down the passage, and perfume from her
cupboard drifts up, to meet and commingle at the place
where she fell.

> *On the clear understanding*
> *that this kind of thing can happen,*
> *shall we dance?*

This must be the place where she fell – the picture frame
cracked and askew – just next to the light switch for the
bathroom. The seismic aftershocks crackle every time I walk
past. Where the weight of her shoulder hit the wall. This is
the place she was struck. Struck down, struck out. A blow
to the head. To the heart. A stroke of luck. A caress of
wings. The strike that put an end to the desolate nights
without him.

> *Zvicha manifesta,*
> *zvicha manifesta.*
> *Ehe zvicha manifesta.*

When did you fall that night, my mother? How long after we spoke on the phone? When did something finally break inside?

Did you sleep? Did you wake late that night or early that morning? Did it happen as you prepared for bed? While you were flossing and brushing? Did it hurt? Were you cold? Where you lay in the passage in the dark?

In the place where you fell. From where you would never get up. Where you lay in the dark with no one to hear you until your brain could no longer breathe.

7 Balfour Road

The dark wooden tea trolley no longer stands
where it should – under the windowsill in the dining room.
The tea tray set, ready, covered with a net.

The windowpane, where daily, the gardener placed
an enormous leaf sliced with a knife from the banana tree.
To save the birds who, should they see through the pane
to the wide lawn and strelitzia tree
on the other side of the house, fly into the glass.

I look through the glass into the dining room, onto the stoep
to the wild green stretch beyond the dark interior.
It is easy to believe you can fly straight through.
It is easy to believe you can fly down the curling driveway
straight through the house to the green beyond.

We found a loerie once, under the window
among the cement flowerpots, green feathers soft
as your hair.

Before the rigor mortis set in, you took it to the National Museum
to be stuffed. To teach the children about such creatures.

The underside of its wings
scarlet as a rush of blood from the brain.

Aftermath

Like a strange new skin
mould grows all over
the carpet left out
on the line in the rain.

The dogs don't mind
if papers pile up
and whisky bottles
come into the bedroom.

Weeds poke up
their little green lives
between gaps
in the paving stones.

Magnitude

She loved the stars, my mother,
said they tested her idea of God.

Not a child joining the dots on the sky's shifting canvas
– but the actual stars:

elemental balls of gas and plasma
living, dying and still being born in their stellar nurseries
inside the dark dusty lanes of the Milky Way

a hive mind of burning light
giving birth to everything that is –

hydrogen to helium
helium to carbon
carbon to oxygen

combustions and combinations
the white hot furnaces of nucleosynthesis.

Imagine it, she would say,
all that activity up there.

They are still working on the question of where
we got the heavy metals – all the gold,
the silver, the platinum, the vanadium.

From the collisions of neutron stars perhaps
or the terminal explosions of massive supernovae.

She worked in the mines when she was young.
Saw the exposed ore running like arteries through host rock.
Until the accident happened and the men said
the spirits were unhappy with a female underground.

So she became a teacher.
I don't know when it was she first started looking up
but she lived long enough to hear the first chirrup
of a gravitational wave

cascading through spacetime like the trace of a stone
still skimming the bendable surface of a lake,
the curved rhythm of rib bones still breathing with a spine.

It took hundreds of scientists over forty years
to design an instrument that sensitive.

She lived long enough to learn that all matter
that moves, leaves its signature behind.

She still chirrups into the atmosphere
of this small spinning planet,
warmed by the light of its third-generation star,

reminds me to see the universe as Einstein chose – as a miracle –
reminds me that the chicken, the kitten,
the msasa trees and their hairy caterpillars are holy.

What happens to a solar system when it loses its brightest star?

Oh Stella by Starlight, I wonder where you are?
Oh Stella by Starlight, I don't think you've gone far.

II

O-o-h Child

O-o-h child,
lifting the record-player arm with a trembling hand,
laying your head next to the speaker.

Your father is at war,
Nixon is a crook, and that naked child
running from the napalmed forest,

out-screaming Munch, is only one of many.
O-o-h child, it's not going to stop,
this wash of death on the shore each morning.

For where can they live?
Refugees crammed into boats.
Homes all wrecked by sonic boom and flame.

Men and women suffocating side by side
in containers on trucks and on ships.
Running out of air in the darkness.

Running away into their airless futures.
O-o-h child, the people can't breathe.
The police are still pressing on their necks.

And just the other day they shot a little boy,
with his pockets full of biscuits,
but no one goes painting his name.

O-o-h child, look around, things aren't going to get easier.
The young never had your kind of hope.
The old ones took for granted

the lake at dusk, flies and fish
rising to the rippled surface.
The beauty of the world unassailable.

Trees still shed enough pollen
on one summer day for a thousand orchards
but there won't be enough bees left to cope.

South Africans Only

Everyday we get more illegal
       – Juan Felipe Herrera

There is a Zimbabwean mother on Bathurst Street.
She is about to board the Greyhound back to Harare.
I know this trip well. It will take her two days. If she's lucky.
She used to work with my dad. We have settled her daughter
into a university residence. It is Orientation Week.
Just before she leaves, she is refused a plastic spoon for her
yoghurt by the woman behind the counter in the KFC because
she cannot reply to a sentence in isiXhosa. Because black as
she is, she is too black or perhaps she is not black enough.
*Because the amakwerekwere are criminals and animals who bring us
disease. Because all they want is to steal our livelihoods, and take
our jobs.*

When the mob attack the spaza shops –
because South Africa does not belong to all who live in it
and what are these people doing here anyway?
They are killing us for muti, they are marrying our women.
Mabahambe! Mabatshise!
They must go! They must burn! –
we spend the night getting the students out.

One by one I fetch them. Handed each address
by the International Office. One by one I find them.
Collect them. Bring them onto campus.
One by one they sit beside me in the passenger seat,
some cowed, some panicked, some angry. Each clutches
a bag, a backpack, sometimes a small suitcase.

Kenya, he says.
Malawi, she says.
Zimbabwe, Harare, she says. *Oh Chisipite Senior School?*
Yes, me too!

I'm actually from Durban, she says. *I'm Zulu but I'm so dark
I'm afraid I'll be mistaken for a Nigerian. I watched them
from my window as they dragged the woman out to the street.
They threw bricks. They climbed on the roof to get inside her shop.
They called her a whore. They took everything.*

The SAPS take five hundred men to safety in a hotel
on the highway. Their wives and children
are left behind.

The young Zimbabwean poet will only come
to the poetry sessions on campus.
He will not join us on the bus when we travel each fortnight
up Jacob Zuma Drive
to the Assumption Development Centre in Joza.
On campus he can read, he is a poet, among poets.
In the kasi, he is not welcome.
So he will not come. *Shamwari, your white skin gives you a pass
I do not get. I will never be one of them. I do not belong.*

Sectioned

A person may be sectioned, under the United Kingdom's Mental Health Act: If a person appears to a constable to be suffering from mental disorder and to be in immediate need of care or control, the constable may, if he thinks it necessary to do so in the interests of that person or for the protection of other persons (a) remove the person to a place of safety within the meaning of section 135, or (b) if the person is already at a place of safety within the meaning of that section, keep the person at that place or remove the person to another place of safety.
– United Kingdom's Mental Health Act, Section 136.

Everyone in here is white, except the nurses.
Everyone in here, except the nurses, has terrible teeth.
English shark-teeth smiles.
Coz the NHS don't ever pay for the dentist, innit?
The nurses are all dark brown. They are calm
in their starched white dresses. More composed than I,
facing this shiver of shark-toothed women
who swim all around me as I walk through the second set
of double-sealed doors with my Tesco plastic bags to bring you
brand new underwear, t-shirts, trackpants, toiletries.
A nurse tries to get them away from me.
Leave me be, you black bitch, snaps a shark-tooth.
You think you so clever.

I've also brought you smokes. A mistake, perhaps.
I've made you the centre of attention and now
you're surrounded. You are breathless. Your eyes
have disappeared down two black holes.

You are wearing the paper panties they gave you
and somebody's smelly jersey. Except

they don't call it a jersey here.
They call it a jumper. Stupid words.
Jumpers. Trainers. Innit?
I want to get you out of this place
where the white women, whose mouths reek
as they talk, think they are better
than the black women they call bitches.

We are smoking on the tiny patch of grass
in the small courtyard.
The wet green grass on which no one can ever sit down.
Not even when it is sunny.
In the windows opposite us on the first floor, the men appear.
All in a row at the tall windows, wanking.
All in a row with their pink cocks out.

Orrr, go on then, big boys, give us a show!
shouts one of the shark-tooths.

The women forget your cigarettes as they crowd to the windows
or out onto the wet grass, whooping and grunting.
This happens every day, you say quietly.
We watch as the men and women separated by a courtyard
grind up against each other across the open air.
The nurses stand silently and watch.

I find the nurse I spoke with on the phone.
She has nothing with her, she said.
She is wearing paper panties.
She needs toiletries, clothes. She needs to see you.
I write down the address, the list. Then I say:
Sister, may I ask something. Are you from Zimbabwe?
A silence on the line.

Why do you ask, she says slowly, at last,
if I am from Zimbabwe?

Because I am from Zimbabwe, I say.
And now I am here, I want to say
to her, to myself, to you,
what is any Zimbabwean doing in a place like this?
But we don't ask. We simply clap our cupped hands
and meet each other's eyes
as the shark-tooths swim around us.

They are small. They are smelly and damp.
The one talking to you now
has grey foam in each corner of her mouth.
But she rounds her vowels and lifts her chin.
She thinks she is better than the black women she calls bitches.
I can almost taste her breath and
there is yellow sleep in the corners of her eyes and
for all the time we smoke outside she stays with us and
clearly she has befriended you and
that terrifies me because I have to leave you here.
I have to bring you back after they release you
into my care to check on your cat, your flat.
I have to make you pinky swear – just like we did as kids –
at the doubled-sealed doors as we step into London,
that you won't run away.
Because there's nowhere to go.

Reggae For Bob

– after Linton Kwesi Johnson
– for Gillian Makura, 1971-2015

We're five little girls. We're just sixteen.
And all the world seems Eden green.
With no shoes, no boys, no rash temptation.
We carry Bob Marley, his songs of redemption.
They swing from one hand on the radio-tape deck.
As we walk through the grass on a Saturday picnic.
Harare City. Botanical Garden.
And all the world seems green and Eden.

When the rain comes falling, it shines in the sun.
When the rain comes falling, it doesn't stop our fun.
When the rain comes falling, we aren't worried getting wet.
When the rain comes falling, we do not feel upset.
It falls soft, like pollen, like tiny golden leaves.
It falls soft, like pollen, like blessing or reprieve.

Only now, my youth long gone,
I think of that day as formation.

Bob Marley and the girls and the golden rain.
It needs a mention.
It needs attention.

For it's part of my brain.
It's part of my brain.
And I want to live the same.
So I'm going to live the same.

Five little black and white girls. We're from Harare.
Our hometown now gone wrong and scary.
We're far from home. We see little good.
And I think of that day from our childhood.

Harare. 1988.
The adults. They're still holding hate.

But in the eighties, when we were lighties.
We had the wise poet's words.
We had the warm pollen rain.
And we felt it the same.
We felt it the same.

So Bob Marley and the girls and the golden rain.
It needs a mention.
It needs attention.
For it's part of our brain.
It's part of our brain.

And we want to live the same.
So we're going to live the same.

When the rain comes falling, it shines in the sun.
When the rain comes falling, it doesn't stop our fun.
When the rain comes falling, we aren't worried getting wet.
When the rain comes falling, we do not feel upset.
It falls soft, like pollen, like tiny golden leaves.
It falls soft, like pollen. Like blessing. Like reprieve.

Line in the Sand

We are in my house. Sitting side by side on the broken second-hand sleeper couch watching Oprah. It is a Tuesday in September, and the cats are at play in the late afternoon grass. I rescue the chameleon they are chasing. He hisses, nips and twists. His rage has turned him a dark purply green. Oprah is telling us, beyond anything she says, that the world can always be put right – that it can be made even better. It is your last night here. I am cooking you a special supper. Herbs and salad from the earth at my feet. You have been here two weeks. Our laughter bouncing in the car as sunflowers, cattle and mountains glide past. I have taken you everywhere. We have been to Robben Island on the boat and back. Felt the cold tiles on the floor of Madiba's cell. Now you are here, in my part of the world, the Eastern Cape. You are here in it with me.

The SABC interrupts Oprah and you are on the phone to your parents in Washington DC. It is still morning there, and you are crying and shouting and asking questions about a friend in New York and suddenly, instead of being afraid for you, I am afraid of you, of something in the tone of your voice, as you sit on the wooden floorboards in the passage. I am afraid of what it will take to assuage your pain. Of what it will take to make you feel safe again. You are unharmed. The people you love are unharmed. But with this first and terrible baptism, wet all over with a splash of its waters, you are incredulous, petulant. Your pain so unbearable because it has never learnt to be modest – to accept the simple fact of a father in uniform taken away in a truck. I begin to step away from you. I go back to the

kitchen, to cook, to breathe. I walk out into the beautiful
light and sit on the bench and smoke. We eat together.
I give you my small FM radio, and you ride through the
night on the Greyhound to Cape Town listening to the reports.

I sit up unsleeping on the broken second-hand sleeper
couch and watch the explosions begin in the night sky over
Kabul. No one knows who is responsible.

I think it is the Americans. I am wrong tonight but I am not
that wrong. It is not the Americans yet, but it will be.
The Americans who are already demanding without saying
in so many words that at least one person must die in
Afghanistan for everyone who died in New York. Maybe not
just in Afghanistan. Maybe double or triple would do it.

We know what is coming. We know we can do nothing to
stop it. We know the heft and taste and smell of it without
yet knowing the details. Those of us who have never been
safe, we know. We have known since we were children not
to trust. Not the government, the police, not a word we read
in the paper. We look on in disbelief as you fall for it all.

Godson

This child and I have only a day
for a beach where we might have spent
a lifetime.

The time itself like one
of these temporary tidal pools,
full for the moment

with rafts of gathered bubbles
patterning the unstill sand,

with the movements of tiny fishes
who flee as we step.

They, like us, dart as one.
Schooling.

We glut on the time.
You want me to watch you
and I want to watch.

Every jump, dive, splash
of your stubby little body.
Look at me! you cry. Calling and calling my name.
And I do.

We will see each other again.
But you will be much changed.
I will be much the same.
Walking here with my dogs.

Look at the shallow dip
on the sand by that rock.

That day it was a pool
where you spent almost an hour
chasing one grey fingerling of a fish
with the glare of their stainless steel bowl.

You kept it, and kept it –
its little fins fanning the tepid water –
until I made you give it back.

So it could live its own life,
in the sea, I said.

Crackdown

It is permanent. Without remorse.
It keeps on happening
and we cannot make it stop. None of us can stop it
and, lord knows, we have tried.

My own father, marching to the Harare High Court
in his black gown and white neckband,
a peaceful lunchtime demonstration
by the Zimbabwe Law Society and
Zimbabwe Lawyers for Human Rights.

They are marching against disappearances. Against deaths
in police custody. Against abductions by state security.
The beating and torture of members of the opposition.
Arrests and assaults on journalists, leaders of labour
and social movements, locked away on spurious charges.
Labelled 'D' for Dangerous. Judges who uphold
their independence need bodyguards.
Lawyers are detained as criminals
to prevent them from acting for their clients.

They are marching for all of us.
Marching for human rights and the rule of law.
Such simple but impossible things.

His tired old arms are orange, green
and bottom-of-the-ocean blue.
The riot police have tattooed him with their batons.
They have inked him a sleeve that says,
No. Never. None of that here.

Blueberries

This little box of blue
in the supermarket fridge
is a miniature scrap of my flag.
PRODUCE OF ZIMBABWE, it declares.
I hold the clear plastic box to my chest.
Stand staring into the fridge
until my shoulders stop heaving.

I take two.
Sit at my kitchen table
and eat an entire bowl straight off.
Bite down into the red soil and rain
of my homeland. Think of the hands that picked them.
People who watered and pruned,
working rows of saplings for two whole years
before pale green bushes bore fruit in the sun.

I know this taste. Nhimbe Fresh.
These grow on Edwin Moyo's farm near Marondera.
These are the OZblu. The largest
sweetest variety in the world. Flown out in cold storage
to markets in Europe and South Africa,
long before the harvest can begin elsewhere.
Why do I care so much?
Nations are stories. Colonial fictions.
Farms are farms. Workers are workers.
They face the same privations the world over.
But I do.

This farmer has recovered. This farmer is exporting!
He's partnering with small-scale growers again.

He offers training and a clinic.
Has plans for tobacco and peas,
stone-fruit and raspberries.

This farmer has risen from the ruin
of his farm, Kondozi. His workers
beaten, evicted at gun point.

The tears come again
as I bite down deep into the blue-black sadness,
taste the dark bittersweet of the diaspora blues.

History Will Break Your Heart

Italicised words are quotations from interviews included in the video installation created by visual artist Kemang wa Lehulere, for his 2015 exhibition History Will Break Your Heart, *which engaged with the life and work of the South African painter, Gladys Mgudlandlu (1917-1979).*

Deep inside a house in Gugulethu,
a river runs underground.

Trees and mountain tops whisper to each other
under nine layers of paint and plaster,
under nine layers of pain.

Stars twinkle but no one sees their glow.

> *The houses in Gugulethu were all identical. You were not allowed to change or add on to your house in any way. When you went into her house, it felt like another kind of house. It moved like a sea snake.*

> *That woman used to paint all the walls in her house. We didn't know it was art.*

> *Something like a river and some fish. You see something greenish like waving reeds and when you turned, rondavels. An old man standing there.*

Deep inside a house in Gugulethu,
a river was painted over in beige.
It should be a national monument.

They have opened up a modest glimpse. A small square
of blackish green. Is it the river? The mountain? The sky?
It is sprinkled with hollow stars where the chisel's tooth bit
down – each blow of the small sharp blade – to lift the paint.

A pipe is broken on either edge of the dream.

> *She claimed herself the first black woman painter*
> *in South Africa. There was quite a lot of attention.*
> *She met with ambassadors from the US.*
> *She exhibited in town.*

She called herself uNontaka, the bird woman, painting
from high up and far away. She died alone and penniless.
Like Ingoapele Madingoane. Like so many others.
Her house sold. Her murals painted over.

> *You could see a rural area in her house.*
> *Perhaps she was missing home. So she drew it.*
> *Maybe it was her home she put there?*

Crypsis

What a difference a leg makes.

The big bullet of your head flecked in scales of shadow,
bronze and grey. Your unblinking eyes black as polished
agate. The flick of your forked tongue both midnight
and lightning, tasting our smell as you fix your stare from
inside the creeper at the top of the house on the dog and me
below, while we stare up. My heart's percussion sounding
through my hands and into the body of the dog as I lift her
straight off the ground, hold her up against my breathless
chest, all the hairs on her back, my arms, standing straight
up, awake, shouting:

Snake! Snake! The heated air around us liquid
as the gathered muscles in your gaze.

A stand-off. I wish I could clone myself. One of me to carry
the dog off to safety in the house and fetch the phone,
the other to stand watch outside lest you vanish, which you do.

The snake-catcher, the clasp at the end of his wooden
walking stick fashioned from the brake of a bike, pokes
at the undergrowth, all along the corrugated iron peeling
away from the wall, until you climb out into the sun
to show yourself:

you are not the biggest puff adder I've ever met but
a leguaan. You climbed up there with your hands, your
claws, stirred from the depths in the damp narrow space
between the buildings when I grabbed at the creeper

and shook, yelled to force the rats towards the waiting dog,
her bark a clear alarm that what I'd shaken loose was more
than vermin.

I watch you stand on my roof until you turn, with fierce
deliberate slowness, to climb back down to your burrow
in the cool dark. I'm so sorry I disturbed your sleep. I flush
with an odd sense of benediction, in your decision to choose
my pond, this wall, this gap between the houses
as your dwelling place. When the snake-catcher leaves,
I go out again, to leave you an egg.

When UNoluthando arrives that week for work, I tell her
over coffee what I've scared up outside, warn her not to go
near that side of the house for a while. *A water leguaan is
living there. A monitor lizard.* She shakes her head a little,
frowns. I google the isiXhosa term.

Uxam, I learn to say at last. *Uxam*, she replies, lets loose
a long, low whistle. *We believe that if Uxam comes to your
house, the ancestors are visiting.*

It was my father's birthday, I say.
Yes, she says. *Uxam*.

Pride

My mother is laughing in the kitchen
and we are all floating on it.
The light-streaked gladness
she shares with these women,
her teacher-training-college friends.

I am sitting in a plastic chair by the pool
with their husbands and my father.
They are gently nursing coals
and turning meat with tongs.

Beers balanced on well-fed bellies,
they blow out smoke and resignation,
as their talk turns to the inevitable.
Runaway inflation, black-market forex,
horror stories from customs and excise,
roadblocks, seizures, shortages, queues.

Then, from the short, handsome one
who'd been a troopie with my father:
*But I do agree with Mugabe about one thing –
and that's his policy on the poofs.*

That's it, I think,
I am never coming back.

But my father shakes his head,
Oh no, come on now. You can't say that.
And he goes on,
weighing and choosing each word,

keeping them light but resolved, precise.
In his best courtroom form.
He speaks of *an extraordinary contribution,*
to society, the arts.
He mentions names:
What about Cole Porter? Or Oscar Wilde? he asks.
Or Noel Coward? Mad Dogs and Englishmen eh?

The other men grunt, look down.
What indeed?
They all shuffle in their seats, get up, check the meat.
While I rub his broad knee and grin.

This will not be his kindest act, certainly.
Nor will these finally count as among his bravest words.
But they are the ones that first made me stop.
Take notice.
Pay better attention,
in reckoning a man I'd known since birth.

Allow me to think as I sit here beside him,
You see this man here?
He's my dad.
Mine.

One Hundred Lesbians

— *after Wisława Szymborska*

When was I last with one hundred lesbians?
One hundred women who love women?

Jozi Pride, 2011.
High as a balloon on E and leaping
for the sky at Zoo Lake.

Lira womans onto the stage
and sings us 'Pata Pata'.
Everyone whoops and stamps.
We leap on the flat dry grass.

One hundred lesbians? More.

Queer women everywhere.
It's as queer as the eye can see.

The shirtless firemen on their float.
The BDSM peeps with their studs and whips.

The thin old white guy who
joins our table in the sun
doesn't say a word.

When we say hello,
he holds up a cardboard sign
that reads 'Born this Way'
and smiles without his teeth.

Me in my new blue jeans
and the dark brown t-shirt
that was a gift from a friend:

*Dip me in chocolate and
throw me to the lesbians.*

Brand new. Freshly hatched.
38 and never been kissed
 – by a girl.

(No. There was that one time,
that truth-or-dare game, that undergrad party.
It made me so afraid of myself).

But here I am at last in my
new blue jeans and my new
chocolate shirt standing in
the queue for the portaloo in
my shweshwe hat.

And a beautiful girl with wide
dark eyes asks me if this is the queue.

When I reply, she smiles and says
Oh you're so cute! Can I give you a kiss?

When I say yes, she kisses each of my cheeks.
Then another girl says, *Oh me too please.*

Suddenly here they are.
Women putting their arms around me.
Oh all the lovely beaming and kissing!

Alone in the portaloo, I can
hardly stand. I look at myself
in the tiny square of mirror
hooked over the basin
on the blue plastic wall.

My face is covered in lipstick.
Kisses in pink, in red, in brown
and purple and green. The pupils
of my eyes are enormous.

I took a selfie of the new
me in a portaloo
at ten past three.
My pupils wide with Ecstasy.

38 and just covered in kiss.
Tell me, who could have pictured this?

So let's take one hundred lesbians.

Those who knew from very young
they were, somehow, different?
Seventy-eight.

Those who knew exactly who they were as children
and became gold star lesbians?
Fifteen, maybe. (Statistics here will depend on the letter
of their generation.)

Those who were tomboys and different from the other girls
but went on to marry a man and have children?
Fifty-eight (maybe more).

Those who never considered themselves queer but one day, to their surprise, found themselves in love with a friend?
Thirty-two.

Those who came out to their families, to be accepted and loved without questions asked?
Two.

Those who were bullied by parents, peers and teachers?
Ninety-eight.

Those who have been raped, harassed or assaulted because they are lesbians?
Fifty-six.

Those who have been raped, harassed or assaulted because they are women?
Eighty-four.

Those who have been with more than one man and wonder if they are permitted to embrace the name of 'lesbian'?
Seventy-seven.

Those who embrace 'queer' as a better term for themselves?
Sixty-three.

Those who sometimes wish they weren't queer?
Thirty-five

Those who feel being queer is the best thing in the world?
Forty-two.

Those who beat themselves up for leaving
it all so goddamn late?
Eighty-nine.

Those who decide to transition to somewhere non-binary or fluid?
Twenty-one.

Those who live with self-hatred that surfaces without warning?
Ninety-eight.

Those for whom it sometimes surfaces, what they really want,
but who've decided it's either too late or too difficult to come out?
Thirty-four.

You cannot take one hundred lesbians and tell their stories in
numbers. All models are subjective.
Besides, I'm a poet, not a mathematician.

At one point, we all might have been any of these women.

Except (of course)
those lucky two.

We Are Mostly Water

They are telling tales of you in Spanish
on both sides of the Atlantic.
On Facebook you have written up a small legend
of your time in Buenos Aires.
Your tattoo, the tango championships,
your appearance on Rock & Pop FM.
A ring for every finger in the street markets.
Strolling under the gaze of the pink house of parliament,
its rose-coloured colonnades once tinted with an ox's blood.

In Grahamstown, the taps went dry for four entire days.
The townsfolk were dirty and mad.
The police brought helmets, shields
and a water cannon to the protest.
In the crowd, one woman suggested inciting a riot,
just to get a shot at the water.

Each day there is only air in the pipes.
How strange, that the absence of water
should sound so like an ocean –
the suck and hiss on a line
as the phone connects across acres of sea.

At dawn I carry buckets from the rain tank.
Warm three large pots on the stove,
squat in the bath like a frog,
and toss them, methodically, over my head.
Wet.
Soap.
Rinse.

My life has made me an artist of bucket baths –
of making the most of very little.
But how I curse the brevity of connection
when all the modest pots of it are done.

As I turn again from chopping board
to empty tap, to rinse my hands,
I think of reaching for yours.
And ponder how it is that water is like love.

We are drenched in it. Steeped.
We play with it, waste it.
An outage brings a reckoning with need.
How deep and vast and recurrent it is.

I know, I know, even now we are connected,
an ocean holds our continents in the crook of each arm.
But I am listening for water in the pipes.
I want to hear the sound of it
gurgling closer to home.

I want to bathe again,
to wallow and luxuriate,
run its little rivulets into all the hollow places,
connect with every inch of my skin.

Thin Line

My father said,

There's a thin line

Between very brave and very stupid.

If it all works out, they'll all say

You were very brave.

But if it doesn't work out, they'll say

You were very stupid.

Old friends are like worn-in coats.

They fit snug.

You fathead!

I know you gannets ate all the fruit.

You're way out past the shark nets.

Come back this instant!

I'm so glad you learnt to drink whisky!

Do you want a little pink in your drink?

Moenie panic nie!

I hate you coz your feet's too big.

You're the giddy limit!

Them's the breaks kids.

If I tell you the truth.

It will be the scariest thing I've done.

Another precipice in the desert.

Another devil tempting me to jump.

If I tell you the truth.

If I tell you.

But aren't I already?

My friends tell me all the time.

Don't wear your heart on your sleeve.

They tell me it's just too funny.

To watch me failing to lie.

My face is my tell.

And it's all written there.

I can't help myself.

There's no hiding this.

It's as big as the moon.

Big silver waterskin.

Full almost to bursting.

Rising right through these curtains.

I Know You Are Reading This Poem

– *after Adrienne Rich*

I know you are reading this poem lying flat on the couch
by the window, aware of the little lizards stalking each other
and leaping about on the wall outside.

I know you are reading this poem smoking in the bath on
a Saturday morning, as the warm air, the words, the smoke,
and your nakedness, mingle and mellow in the steam.

I know you are reading this poem in the sun on the stoep
of an old Karoo house in the winter, having driven so far
to escape your own life and yet facing it here on the page.

I know you are reading this poem on the computer in your
office instead of working because you need something else
today to help you chart a way through.

I know you are reading this poem on the small screen
of your phone in the middle of the night, shaken by a dream
in which you embraced your lost lover.

I know you are reading this poem among strangers
on a train as you rattle towards an unfamiliar city you
are learning to loathe.

I know you are reading this poem on the windowsill
of a hotel room in summer as the women on the roofs nearby
hang washing and laugh with each other.

I know you are reading this poem under your breath
between bookshelves in a chain store, because you need
to remember who you are, and you can't afford the book.

I know you are reading this poem in a language not your
own but one in which you write, often dream, and also
sometimes make love.

I know you are reading this poem at a table in the public
library, because you are lonely and homesick for your
own country, to which you may never return.

I know you are reading this poem because you don't know
anyone else who feels like this and yet here are the echoes
of your own private yearnings.

I know you are reading this poem because you need it near
you always, a strand in the rope that drew you, hand over
hand, out of the well.

The Song of Deborah

I didn't want to be the prophet under a palm tree,
dispensing counsel to citizens and warriors.

I liked the other woman, Jael,
who snuck back into the tent that night
to hammer a peg into the forehead of the enemy general
while he slept off the battle and her gift of the milk.

Don't worry about me, I'd say.
I was named after a woman who drove a tent peg
into a guy's head, I'm going to be fine.

But I wasn't. I was named after the other one.
When I saw my mistake, I was disappointed.

I'm still growing into this name.
The wide open door in the capital D.
The walk tall stretch of the b and the h.

I sit in the shade of the consonants,
like she sat under her tree.

My work is to teach the young people.
I want each of them to live their own lives
and well.

Acknowledgements

Thanks are due to the editors of the following publications in which versions of some of these poems first appeared: *Botsotso*, *New Contrast*, *Ons Klyntji*, *Sinister Wisdom* and the *Gerald Kraak Anthology vol. III: The Heart of the Matter*. Thank you to my many masahwira, who read these poems with me as they were written and for all their insight and advice.

Deborah Seddon

Notes on Poems and Quotations

Phrases and quotations have been used, sometimes with and sometimes without acknowledgement.

Page vii

Perhaps home is not a place but simply an irrevocable condition
The epigraph to the collection is taken from James Baldwin's novel *Giovanni's Room* (New York: Dial Press, 1956).

Page 7

'Harare City, Sunshine City' takes its title from the nickname given to the capital of Zimbabwe. EcoCash is a mobile phone-based money transfer service, launched in 2011 by Econet Wireless, and used widely to manage almost all transactions in Zimbabwean Dollars. This is because local bank notes and coins are in very short supply, and there are no working ATMS. At the time of writing, Zimbabwe uses two currencies: the mostly virtual Zimbabwean Dollar and the US Dollar in cold hard cash.

Page 12

Again-est is Zimbabwean slang for being stubborn or contrary.

Page 14

Masahwira is the ChiShona word for the friends who are as close as family. *Sekuru* is the ChiShona word for uncle or grandfather, also used as a term of respect when addressing any man who is older than the speaker.

Page 19

Swing low, sweet chariot, coming for to carry me home borrows a line from "Swing Low," one of the best known African-American spirituals.

Page 32

'How Long Has This Been Going On?' takes its title from one my father's favourite songs by George and Ira Gershwin (1928).

Page 34

'Baba' takes its title from the ChiShona word for father. The poem borrows lyrics from 'The Hippopotamus Song' in Michael Flanders and Donald Swann's album *At the Drop of a Hat* (1957); the jazz standard 'How About You?' written by Burton Lane and Ralph Freed (1941); 'Buona Sera' by Louis Prima and his Orchestra (1957); and Louis Armstrong's 'Shadrack' in *Louis and the Good Book* (1958).

Page 37

'Someday I'll Love Deborah Seddon' is after Ocean Vuong's poem 'Someday I'll Love Ocean Vuong' from his collection *Night Sky with Exit Wounds* (2017), which, in turn, is after Roger Reeves, after Frank O'Hara.

Page 44

'No Mama, No Papa, No Whisky Soda' borrows from a range of sources and uses ChiShona, one of the two major indigenous languages in Zimbabwe.
Penga is the ChiShona word for crazy.

Chigub is Zimbabwean slang for a petrol container (the word alludes to the pouring sound).

I heard somebody say / Burn, baby, burn. Disco inferno / Burn, baby, burn. Burn that mother down is borrowed from the song 'Disco Inferno' by the Trammps from their 1976 album of the same name.

Firestarter (1980) and *Cujo* (1981) are novels by Stephen King and are referenced in this poem.

Maswera sei? Taswera kana maswerawo is a ChiShona greeting that translates to 'How did you spend your day? I spent my day well if you spent your day well'.

She's crazy like a fool / What about Daddy Cool? is from the Boney M song 'Daddy Cool' in their debut album *Take the Heat Off Me* (1976).

Maiwe! is a ChiShona exclamation of distress and surprise, akin to the English word 'alas'.

Ndinopenga. Tinopenga. Maningi sterrek! is ChiShona for 'I am crazy, we are crazy, too much so'. (*Sterrek* is Zimbabwean slang adapted from the Afrikaans word *sterk* for strong.)

Hey kid, would you like a Hershey bar? So would I is a quotation from J.G. Ballard's *Empire of the Sun* (1984).

But I cannot choose but weep, / to think they should lay him i' the cold ground are words spoken by Ophelia in Shakespeare's *Hamlet*.

Awake, awake, Deborah!/ Awake, awake, utter a song! is from 'The Song of Deborah' in the Book of Judges in the King James Version of the Bible.

They all fall down is a line from the song 'Ring a Ring o Roses', which was made popular around 1665 during the Great Plague of London.

Hondo is the ChiShona word for war.

Sadza is the ChiShona term for a porridge made from maize meal. It is a staple food in Zimbabwe but there are frequent shortages.

No Twitter? No WhatsApp? Get a VPN references the blocking of social-media platforms in Zimbabwe during times of protest or stay-aways. The easiest way to avoid the Internet blockades is to

download a free Virtual Private Network, well before they happen.
How do you hold a moonbeam / in your hand? is borrowed from the song 'Maria' in the film *The Sound of Music* (1965).
On the clear understanding / that this kind of thing can happen/ shall we dance? is borrowed from the song 'Shall We Dance' in the film *The King and I* (1956).
Zvicha manifesta, / zvicha manifesta / Ehe zvicha manifesta is borrowed from the song 'Sahwira' (a ChiShona term for a friend as close as family) by the Zimbabwean rapper Holy Ten (Mukudzei Chitsama) in his album *Risky Life* (2021). The words translate as 'it will manifest, it will manifest, yes, it will manifest'.

Page 53

'Stella by Starlight' is a jazz standard, originally written by Victor Young for the film *The Uninvited* (1944).

Page 57

'O-o-h Child' takes its title from the name of the song by the Five Stairsteps in their album *Step by Step by Step* (1970).

Page 59

Everyday we get more illegal is the title of a poem by Juan Felipe Herrera, the 21st U.S. Poet Laureate (2015-2017), in his collection of the same name (2020)
Shamwari is the ChiShona word for a friend or an ally.

Page 64

'Reggae for Bob' is inspired by the dub poetry of Linton Kwesi Johnson, particularly 'Reggae fi Dada' in his collection *Mi Revalueshanary Fren: Selected Poems* (2002).

Page 79

'One Hundred Lesbians' is after Wisława Szymborska's 'A Word on Statistics' in her collection *Miracle Fair* (2002).

Page 86

'Thin Line' quotes from Fats Waller's song 'Your Feet's Too Big' (1939).

Page 87

'I Know You Are Reading this Poem' takes up an idea from Adrienne Rich's poem 'An Atlas of the Difficult World' in her collection of the same name (1991).

Page 89

'The Song of Deborah' takes its title from 'The Song of Deborah' in the Book of Judges 5: 2–31, as sung by Deborah and Barak.

Deborah Seddon was born and raised in Harare, Zimbabwe, before emigrating to South Africa where she now lives and works. She is currently a Senior Lecturer in the Department of Literary Studies in English at Rhodes University. Deborah holds a Master of Arts in Creative Writing from Rhodes University and a PhD in English from Cambridge University. During her career as an academic, she has contributed essays, book chapters, articles and reviews to a wide variety of academic publications. Her poetry has been published in various journals both locally and abroad. Her poems have been shortlisted for the *Gerald Kraak Award* and the *National Poetry Prize*. *Magnitude* is her debut poetry collection.

OTHER WORKS BY DRYAD PRESS

THE DRYAD PRESS LIVING POETS SERIES

Not This Tender, Sarah Uheida
earth-circuit, iyra e m maharaj
Night Transit, P. R. Anderson
Dark Horse, Michèle Betty
Star Reverse, Linda Ann Strang
Transcontinental Delay, Simon van Schalkwyk
The Mountain Behind the House, Kobus Moolman
In Praise of Hotel Rooms, Fiona Zerbst
catalien, Oliver Findlay Price
Allegories of the Everyday, Brian Walter
Otherwise Occupied, Sally Ann Murray
Landscapes of Light and Loss, Stephen Symons
An Unobtrusive Vice, Tony Ullyatt
A Private Audience, Beverly Rycroft
Metaphysical Balm, Michèle Betty

OTHER PUBLISHED WORKS

The Creative Arts: On Practice, Making & Meaning,
edited by Michèle Betty & Sally Ann Murray
Palimpsests, Chris Mann
River Willows: Senryū from Lockdown, Tony Ullyatt
missing, Beverly Rycroft
The Coroner's Wife: Poems in Translation,
Joan Hambidge
Unearthed: A Selection of the Best Poems of 2016,
edited by Joan Hambidge and Michèle Betty

Available in South Africa from better bookstores
nationwide and online at www.dryadpress.co.za
and internationally from African Books Collective
(www.africanbookscollective.com)